Mindful
COLOURING
BY NUMBERS
for kids

Buster Books

T0018313

Illustrated by Sarah Wade

Written and edited by Emma Taylor
Cover designed by Angie Allison
Designed by Zoe Bradley & Jade Moore

First published in Great Britain in 2022 by Buster Books, an imprint of
Michael O'Mara Books Limited, 9 Lion Yard, Tremadoc Road, London SW4 7NQ

W www.mombooks.com/buster   F Buster Books   🐦 @BusterBooks   📷 @buster_books

ISBN: 978-1-78055-825-7

1 3 5 7 9 10 8 6 4 2

This book was printed in May 2022 by
Shenzhen Wing King Tong Paper Products Co. Ltd.,
Shenzhen, Guangdong, China.

FSC
www.fsc.org
MIX
Paper | Supporting
responsible forestry
FSC® C010256

Introduction

Mindfulness is all about slowing down and taking the time to notice the small details around you.

By focussing on colouring you can relax and stop thinking too much about all of the things that are worrying you.

Simply follow the number code at the bottom of every page to complete the picture. On most of the pages, you'll notice blank shapes that don't have any numbers inside – these should be left white.

Take your time and enjoy colouring in these joyful and soothing scenes.

Breathe

Mindful breathing can help calm your mind and
body when you're feeling frustrated or upset.

Take a deep breath in through your nose,
like you're smelling the scent of a flower.
Then, breathe out through your mouth
like you're blowing a bubble.

1 = light purple   2 = red   3 = dark green   4 = yellow   5 = light green   6 = pink
7 = orange   8 = dark purple   9 = turquoise   10 = dark blue   11 = light blue   12 = brown

1 = light purple 2 = red 3 = dark green 4 = yellow 5 = light green 6 = pink

7 = orange   8 = dark purple   9 = turquoise   10 = dark blue   11 = light blue   12 = brown

Try Something New

Trying new things can boost your confidence.
It could be learning a new skill, such as baking
or painting. With practice and patience
you'll achieve something great.

1 = light purple   2 = red   3 = dark green   4 = yellow   5 = light green   6 = pink
7 = orange   8 = dark purple   9 = turquoise   10 = dark blue   11 = light blue   12 = brown

1 = light purple   2 = red   3 = dark green   4 = yellow   5 = light green   6 = pink

7 = orange   8 = dark purple   9 = turquoise   10 = dark blue   11 = light blue   12 = brown

Step Outside

Spending time in nature can help you relax.
Step outside and listen to the birds chirping
or insects buzzing. Focus on watching
and listening to them for a while.

1 = light purple   2 = red   3 = dark green   4 = yellow   5 = light green   6 = pink
7 = orange   8 = dark purple   9 = turquoise   10 = dark blue   11 = light blue   12 = brown

1 = light purple 2 = red 3 = dark green 4 = yellow 5 = light green 6 = pink

7 = orange   8 = dark purple   9 = turquoise   10 = dark blue   11 = light blue   12 = brown

Falling Asleep

Everyone struggles to fall asleep sometimes.
At night, thoughts and worries can seem
bigger than they really are.

A warm bath or a gentle stretch
can relax your muscles and help
you wind down for bedtime.

1 = light purple   2 = red   3 = dark green   4 = yellow   5 = light green   6 = pink
7 = orange   8 = dark purple   9 = turquoise   10 = dark blue   11 = light blue   12 = brown

1 = light purple   2 = red   3 = dark green   4 = yellow   5 = light green   6 = pink

7 = orange   8 = dark purple   9 = turquoise   10 = dark blue   11 = light blue   12 = brown

Helping Others

Helping others can give you a sense of purpose
and make you feel good about yourself. It also
helps you to connect with other people
as it shows you care about them.

You don't always need a reason to help someone.
Sometimes it's nice just to make people smile.

1 = light purple   2 = red   3 = dark green   4 = yellow   5 = light green   6 = pink
7 = orange   8 = dark purple   9 = turquoise   10 = dark blue   11 = light blue   12 = brown

1 = light purple   2 = red   3 = dark green   4 = yellow   5 = light green   6 = pink

7 = orange   8 = dark purple   9 = turquoise   10 = dark blue   11 = light blue   12 = brown

Music

Listening to music can quickly boost your mood.
Try making a playlist with all of your favourite
songs so that you can listen to them when
you're feeling worried or upset.

Listen to the beat, the melody and the words.
How do they make you feel?

1 = light purple   2 = red   3 = dark green   4 = yellow   5 = light green   6 = pink
7 = orange   8 = dark purple   9 = turquoise   10 = dark blue   11 = light blue   12 = brown

1 = light purple   2 = red   3 = dark green   4 = yellow   5 = light green   6 = pink

7 = orange   8 = dark purple   9 = turquoise   10 = dark blue   11 = light blue   12 = brown

Be Patient

Changes can happen at any time in your life, and sometimes they can be hard to accept. Always give yourself plenty of time to adjust and remember that change can bring lots of wonderful possibilities and new opportunities.

1 = light purple   2 = red   3 = dark green   4 = yellow   5 = light green   6 = pink
7 = orange   8 = dark purple   9 = turquoise   10 = dark blue   11 = light blue   12 = brown

1 = light purple   2 = red   3 = dark green   4 = yellow   5 = light green   6 = pink

7 = orange   8 = dark purple   9 = turquoise   10 = dark blue   11 = light blue   12 = brown

Move Your Body

Exercise is great for staying fit, but it's important for your mental wellbeing, too. You may find that going for a stroll in the park helps clear your mind and ease your worries.

1 = light purple   2 = red   3 = dark green   4 = yellow   5 = light green   6 = pink
7 = orange   8 = dark purple   9 = turquoise   10 = dark blue   11 = light blue   12 = brown

1 = light purple 2 = red 3 = dark green 4 = yellow 5 = light green 6 = pink

7 = orange 8 = dark purple 9 = turquoise 10 = dark blue 11 = light blue 12 = brown

Comfort

Simple acts of affection, such as a hug, can release chemicals in the brain that make you feel safe and calm. They can also make you feel closer to the people you love.

1 = light purple   2 = red   3 = dark green   4 = yellow   5 = light green   6 = pink
7 = orange   8 = dark purple   9 = turquoise   10 = black   11 = light blue   12 = brown

1 = light purple   2 = red   3 = dark green   4 = yellow   5 = light green   6 = pink

7 = orange   8 = dark purple   9 = turquoise   10 = dark blue   11 = light blue   12 = brown

Reading

Reading is a great way to take a break from your busy day. It's your chance to let go of any distracting thoughts and to concentrate on enjoying a good story. Notice how your worries seem to melt away as you turn the pages.

1 = light purple   2 = red   3 = dark green   4 = yellow   5 = light green   6 = pink
7 = orange   8 = dark purple   9 = turquoise   10 = dark blue   11 = light blue   12 = brown

1 = light purple   2 = red   3 = dark green   4 = yellow   5 = light green   6 = pink

7 = orange   8 = dark purple   9 = turquoise   10 = dark blue   11 = light blue   12 = brown

Do Something Different

Doing things differently can help you to see the world in a different way. It could be something as simple as sitting in a different seat on the bus on the way to school. You may spot things out of the window that you haven't seen before.

1 = light purple 2 = red 3 = dark green 4 = yellow 5 = light green 6 = pink
7 = orange 8 = dark purple 9 = turquoise 10 = dark blue 11 = light blue 12 = brown

1 = light purple   2 = red   3 = dark green   4 = yellow   5 = light green   6 = pink

7 = orange   8 = dark purple   9 = turquoise   10 = dark blue   11 = light blue   12 = brown

One Step at a Time

Life can feel overwhelming sometimes.
When it does, it's best to try focussing on one
thing at a time. While you're busy colouring this
mandala, notice how your thoughts
start to settle.

1 = light purple   2 = red   3 = dark green   4 = yellow   5 = light green   6 = pink
7 = orange   8 = dark purple   9 = turquoise   10 = dark blue   11 = light blue   12 = brown

1 = light purple   2 = red   3 = dark green   4 = yellow   5 = light green   6 = pink

7 = orange   8 = dark purple   9 = turquoise   10 = dark blue   11 = light blue   12 = brown

Happy Place

Where's your favourite place? It could be somewhere you've been on holiday, a place you like to go with a friend or family member, or perhaps it's a room in your house. When you're feeling sad, imagine you're there – remember the smells, the sounds and the things you can see. Thinking about this special place can make you feel calmer and happier.

1 = light purple   2 = red   3 = dark green   4 = yellow   5 = light green   6 = pink
7 = orange   8 = dark purple   9 = turquoise   10 = dark blue   11 = light blue   12 = brown

1 = light purple   2 = red   3 = dark green   4 = yellow   5 = light green   6 = pink

7 = orange   8 = dark purple   9 = turquoise   10 = dark blue   11 = light blue   12 = brown

Meditation

Meditation is about paying attention to what is happening in the moment and tuning into your senses. Ask yourself, how do you feel? What can you see, smell and hear? Practising this for just 5 minutes a day can help you to slow down and feel more relaxed.

1 = light purple   2 = red   3 = dark green   4 = yellow   5 = light green   6 = pink
7 = orange   8 = dark purple   9 = turquoise   10 = dark blue   11 = light blue   12 = brown

1 = light purple   2 = red   3 = dark green   4 = yellow   5 = light green   6 = pink

7 = orange   8 = dark purple   9 = turquoise   10 = dark blue   11 = light blue   12 = brown

Relationships

Good relationships with friends and family are important because they can bring support at the times you need it. Leaning on each other when you're feeling sad or worried can make your troubles seem less overwhelming.

1 = light purple   2 = red   3 = dark green   4 = yellow   5 = light green   6 = pink
7 = orange   8 = dark purple   9 = turquoise   10 = dark blue   11 = light blue   12 = brown

1 = light purple   2 = red   3 = dark green   4 = yellow   5 = light green   6 = pink

7 = orange   8 = dark purple   9 = turquoise   10 = dark blue   11 = light blue   12 = brown

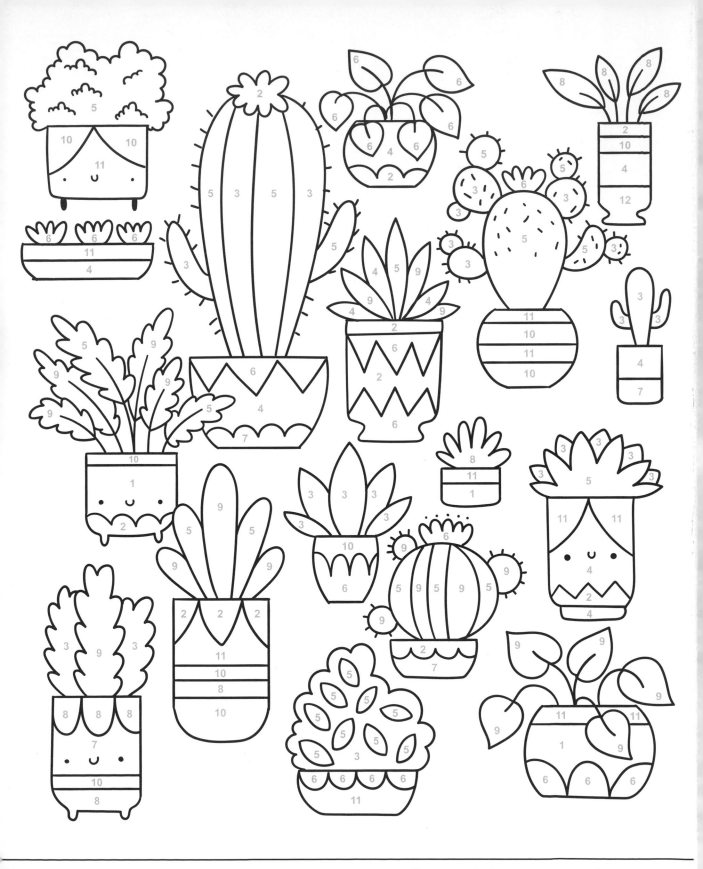

1 = light purple   2 = red   3 = dark green   4 = yellow   5 = light green   6 = pink
7 = orange   8 = dark purple   9 = turquoise   10 = dark blue   11 = light blue   12 = brown